The Renaissance Kids

By Suzanne Weyn
Illustrated by Linda Graves

CELEBRATION PRESS
Pearson Learning Group

Contents

Chapter 1
A Strange Sound

"That's a great costume!" Diana told Matt. "What made you decide to come dressed as a peasant?"

Every year, Putnam Valley Middle School's sixth grade created a Renaissance Fair. With tremendous effort, the students made their cafeteria resemble an English town at the end of the 1500s.

"I thought it was the easiest costume to put together," Matt said. "My mom helped make the shirt, hat, and pants. I just added boots and a vest."

Matt looked Diana up and down. "You look as if you should be running your own castle! Where did you get your costume?"

Diana grinned. "I discovered it in the costume box at home. It's from last year when my sister was in *Romeo and Juliet*."

Behind Matt and Diana, their English teacher, Mrs. Hill, stood in front of a tall cardboard castle. She was dressed as a noblewoman in a long gown with puffed sleeves. Diana nudged Matt and smiled. The teacher's high, pointed hat was threatening to tip over and tumble from her head.

Renaissance-style food was being served around the cafeteria by sixth graders dressed as serving people in white aprons and floppy caps. One stand had turkey drumsticks and beef kebobs. Another offered something called frumenty, which looked like a hot pudding made from cereal.

A boy dressed in knight's armor made of foil and cardboard passed them. He was banging two blocks together to imitate the clip-clop sound of a horse's hooves.

A red ball landed between Matt and Diana. "I need a little help, please," called a girl dressed in a jester's colorful outfit.

Diana scooped up the ball and tossed it back to the jester. "Jessie should learn to juggle one of these days," she said with a laugh.

They walked to a nearby table where some students had built a model of a Renaissance theater. Matt knelt to get an eye-level view of the circular theater built from thin wood.

"This must have taken a long time to build," he

said. "Look at all the little details, like the windows and all the woodwork."

"They left the middle empty," Diana pointed out, peering down into the center of the replica. "Oh, I see. There's the stage, and there's an open area around it." She read aloud from the index card taped to the model. "'This is a model of the Globe Theatre, which opened in 1599. The famed playwright William Shakespeare was part owner of this very popular theater, and many of his most famous plays were performed here. He also acted in some of them.'"

"Whoever built this will definitely get a good grade," Matt remarked.

"Imagine seeing one of Shakespeare's plays in the real Globe Theatre," Diana, who wanted to be an actress, said dreamily. "That would really be something."

"I have trouble following those plays. Why don't they just speak normal English?" Matt said.

Diana laughed. "That *was* normal English to Shakespeare. It's how everyone in England talked back then."

They strolled to the refreshment section and each picked up a drumstick. "Too greasy," Diana said.

Matt wiped his chin. "I like it," he said. "But if you don't, wash it down with some punch."

Diana accepted a cup of greenish punch that a girl scooped from a carved bowl with a wide, wooden ladle. Diana sipped the concoction and then grimaced. "It's so sour! I need water!"

She hurried out of the cafeteria, heading for the water fountain in the hall. Matt followed her into the hall and found her bent over the fountain, drinking great gulps of water.

Diana suddenly stood and tilted her head to one side, listening. "What's wrong?" Matt asked. "What do you hear?"

"Listen. What's that strange sound?" she asked.

Matt listened and slowly nodded. From somewhere down the hall, he could hear someone rattling a

6

locker—but he didn't see anyone there.

"What's making that sound?" Diana wondered as the rattling turned into banging.

"Someone's stuck inside a locker!" Matt said. They raced down the hall and stopped in front of one of the lockers in the long row. The banging sound was definitely coming from inside.

Diana pointed to the dial on the locker door. "We'll never get it open without the combination!"

"Hold on, kid," Matt shouted to the person inside. "We'll get you out. What's your locker combination?"

"What do you mean? Am I dreaming here in the dark?" the person in the locker replied. "For we are such stuff as dreams are made on."

Diana leaned in close to Matt. "He's taking this Renaissance Fair way too seriously," she whispered.

Matt bit his lip to keep from laughing.

"Come on, kid. We're trying to help. Quit fooling around," Matt said. "What's your combination?"

"I wish not to be a fool, for a fool and his money are soon parted," the voice replied.

"We'll have to get a custodian," Matt said.

"Wait a minute. Sometimes people leave the dial set near the last number." Diana gave the dial a light twirl and heard a click. She opened the door. Then she and Matt stepped back in amazement.

A man climbed out of the locker. His long hair receded from a broad forehead. He had a mustache and a neatly trimmed beard.

There was no doubt that the man was dressed for the Renaissance Fair. He wore a richly decorated shirt. His knee-length striped breeches ballooned out over long white stockings. Matt and Diana exchanged confused looks.

"Who *is* he?" Matt muttered. The man was dressed for the fair, so he was probably a teacher, but they had never seen him before. How on Earth had he gotten stuck inside a student's locker?

The man turned in a circle, looking at the school as though he'd never seen one before. "Tell me, is this Sir Walter Raleigh's new world?"

"What did you say?" Matt asked.

"Excuse us a moment," Diana told him as she put her hand on Matt's elbow and drew him a few steps away. "He doesn't know where he is," she whispered.

"Maybe he hit his head on the way to the fair, and now he has amnesia," Matt suggested.

"Then he just fell into a locker?" Diana questioned doubtfully. "Let's find a teacher."

Matt shrugged as he walked back to the man. "Sir, I think you should come inside and talk to our teacher, Mrs. Hill."

The man tilted his head, appearing puzzled. "O brave new world that has such people in it! Do I hear you correctly? You wish me to speak to a missing hill?"

"No, that's not what I meant," Matt said.

"Pray then, I beg you to speak plain English."

Diana smiled, remembering Matt's earlier complaint about Shakespeare. "Matt, let's get Mrs. Hill and introduce her to our friend here."

"Good idea," Matt said. They hurried back into the cafeteria. Mrs. Hill had strayed away from her spot in front of the cardboard castle.

As they looked around, hoping to find her, the stranger from the locker entered the room and began wandering among the crowd. The man saw Matt and Diana and waved for them to join him.

"What *is* this occasion?" he asked when they went to his side. "Who are these youthful workers? Is this the sort of fair held in the new world in your time? Tell me what is happening. I am here to find out all I can about this place."

Once again, Matt and Diana exchanged a confused glance. "It's our Renaissance Fair," Matt explained. "This is an English village in the 1500s."

The man threw his head back and roared with riotous laughter. "Surely you jest," he said. "This is nothing at all like an English village!"

"What? It is so like an English village," Diana argued. "We did a lot of research on what life was like during Queen Elizabeth's reign. She was England's greatest ruler, you know."

"She is indeed, my dear young lady," the man said. "But I'm afraid this is but a pale-blooded imitation of Queen Elizabeth's vibrant age!"

Diana put her hands to her hips. "That's your opinion, maybe, but what makes you an expert?"

"Just take a look in that storage compartment I was locked inside. You'll see something that will prove to you the veracity of my statement."

Just then, Diana noticed Mrs. Hill walking through the crowd, munching on a turkey drumstick. She nudged Matt. He waved to the teacher, but Mrs. Hill didn't see him. Before Matt could catch her attention, she had stepped out into the hall.

"Uh . . . okay," Matt said. "We'll take a look at that locker." To Diana, he whispered, "We've got to catch Mrs. Hill! If we miss her, we'll tell some other adult about this guy." Diana nodded.

The man walked directly to the locker. Matt and Diana lagged behind. "Mrs. Hill!" they hissed, but the teacher was too far ahead of them to hear.

The man threw the locker door open wide. "Take a look for yourself!" he said. "What I wish to show is in this locker."

"No, thanks," Diana said, stepping backward.

"Me neither," Matt said.

"Be not fretful or concerned," the man said. "I will be first to step within."

With that, he bent and stepped into the locker. A strange mist swirled around him. As soon as he had stepped all the way inside, he vanished.

Matt and Diana stared, open-mouthed. "Where did he go?" Matt said. He peered into the locker and waved his hand inside the mist. Instantly he felt as though a powerful suction was pulling him into the locker.

"Matt!" Diana shouted, grabbing his hand. Then she suddenly pitched forward as though she, too, were being sucked inside the locker by an invisible vacuum.

GO COUGARS!

⌁ Chapter 2 ⌁
Through the Time Portal

The locker shook violently. Matt and Diana felt very strange, as if their molecules were being rearranged. Then the locker stopped moving and the mist cleared. They were in a dark container.

"We're back in the locker," Diana said.

"There's no way we'd both fit in there," Matt argued. He felt around for a handle. Then someone opened the door from the outside.

Matt and Diana peered at a gray stone wall. They stepped out and faced the strange man they'd met back at the school. Turning, they saw that they'd been in a large, empty wardrobe—a free-standing closet.

Matt felt it was time to get to the point. "Who *are* you?" he asked.

"*Where* are we?" Diana added.

The man made a sweeping bow. "William Shakespeare at your service."

"No way!" Matt cried.

"Yes, indeed, there is a way," Shakespeare assured him. "You have traveled through time and space, thanks to a most useful time device. You are in the castle of Lord and Lady Overdone."

"A time device? He means a time machine!" Diana whispered to Matt.

They studied the large, beautifully carved, wooden wardrobe. Inside, they saw that a small panel at the bottom displayed a date. It was the exact date of the sixth-grade Renaissance Fair.

"Where did this thing come from?" Matt asked.

"I know not for certain," Shakespeare replied. "Though I hear tell that it was once owned by Leonardo da Vinci, the great artist and inventor." He pointed to an elaborate L etched into the bottom of the wardrobe. "It would require a mind such as his to invent such a remarkable thing. Luckily, I stumbled upon it years ago when my acting company performed here."

"Wait a minute," Diana said. "Are you telling me that *Leonardo da Vinci* once owned this? Didn't he die in the early 1500s?"

"Yes, my lady. Now I must be on my way, for my acting company is in the midst of a crisis." He shut the wardrobe doors and did something to them that Matt and Diana couldn't see. Then he rapped sharply on one of the stones in the wall. A door swung open, and he dashed out.

"Wait!" Diana called, but he was already gone.

"Oh, great!" Matt cried. "Now what?"

"As long as we're here, we might as well look

around," Diana suggested. "Do you think we're really in a castle?"

"I guess we'll find out," Matt said. "But it's pretty weird, don't you think? Could he really be William Shakespeare? That would mean we traveled hundreds of years back in time to the real Renaissance England!"

Diana said, "I don't get it, either. But at least we're dressed for the occasion. We'll fit right in."

They stared at the stone wall. "Which stone did he hit?" Matt asked.

"I have no idea." They began banging on all the stones. It took nearly ten minutes, but the door finally swung open, and they stepped into a long tunnel. When the door closed behind them, the tunnel was thrown into total darkness.

They groped along the hall, feeling their way, until a line of light appeared along the floor. "I guess this is what people mean when they say there's a light at the end of the tunnel," Matt said.

"I'm glad to see it," Diana admitted. "This darkness is creepy."

At the end of the tunnel, they could see a door handle in the dim light. Matt turned it and pulled, but nothing happened. He tried pushing instead. The door swung forward, but only slightly.

"What's pushing back?" Matt asked, alarmed.

Diana peeked around him. "It's a big blanket. Push harder. I'll help." In a second, the door was open wide enough for them to slip out.

"It's one of those wall hangings—a tapestry," Matt pointed out. The large fabric artwork that hid the door showed a woman patting a unicorn.

"How did Shakespeare ever find the hidden door behind this thing?" Matt wondered aloud.

"He's a true Renaissance Man," Diana said. "You know that expression to describe someone with lots of varied talents? That's Shakespeare."

"You there!" a shrill voice bellowed. A broad woman in a lacy cap and a wide skirt was barreling toward them, waving one arm in the air. "Attend to me. Attend to me at once!"

"What do we do?" Matt asked.

"Attend to her, I guess," Diana said.

"Why are you strolling about the castle when there is so much work to be done?" she shouted as she grabbed hold of Diana's shoulders and studied her. "You must be the girl Lady de Cortez sent to be my new lady-in-waiting. What is your name, child?"

"Diana Gonzalez."

"Lady Diana of Gonzalez?"

"Ah—yes, that's right," Diana said.

"I suppose you'll do," Lady Overdone said rudely. She turned to Matt. "I perceive from your clothing that you are the new stable boy. Get out to the courtyard immediately. There is no time to dally. Shoo!" She waved her hands, and Matt had no choice but to head in that direction.

"Now come along," she said to Diana. "I want you to help me find the perfect way to style my hair, for it is not every week that the queen visits us. I, Lady Overdone, must look my best for the queen!"

"The queen?" Diana asked. "Queen Elizabeth?"

"You ridiculous child!" the woman scolded. "What other queen could I possibly mean? Her Royal Majesty values the loyalty of her people, and she never wants to be far from them. She travels throughout her kingdom from time to time, to stay close to her subjects. She refers to these journeys as her progresses, and her travels this week will bring her to our castle."

Silently Matt thanked his mother for insisting he take horseback riding lessons. The moment he'd walked into the castle courtyard, he'd been grabbed by the stable master and told to help groom the horses. He shivered as he worked. It had been winter at home, and it was the same season here, too.

While Matt brushed a huge, brown mare, a short, round man in a velvet cape and hat strode into the stable. "Who has seen William Shakespeare?" he demanded gruffly. "He was here a moment ago."

Matt stepped forward. "He went off to join his acting company," he told the man.

"How *dare* he depart from me, Lord Overdone, without so much as a farewell?" the man shouted. "You, lad, run and fetch him back to my castle. Seek him at the Theatre outside London."

"How will I get there?" Matt asked. "I guess there's no public transportation. Can I borrow a horse?"

"How strangely you speak," Lord Overdone commented. "No, you may not use a horse. You are an able-bodied young servant. You will travel on foot. It should take you no longer than two days."

"Two days!" Matt cried. "On foot?"

"Have you no wits? Of course, on foot! Go, now, unless you wish to be dismissed! Tell Master Shakespeare to return in all haste with his acting company, The Lord Chamberlain's Men. Nothing pleases our good queen more than a play."

"But . . . but . . . I don't have any money," Matt stammered.

Lord Overdone flipped him a small silver coin. "Here is a farthing to buy some bread. You can sleep by the road on the way."

"I'm out of here," Matt said as he ran from the stable. He had no intention of going out to look for Shakespeare.

He slipped into the castle through a side door, determined to find Diana. He walked through a kitchen and out into a wide hall.

"Matt!" Diana called as she ran down the hall toward him. "Let's get out of here! That Lady Overdone is horrible! She keeps making me pin up her hair and then screaming at me that I've done it wrong. I'm going crazy!"

"Me, too," Matt agreed. "Lord Overdone wants me to take a two-day walk to London! No way!"

"We have to find the time machine," Diana said. "Come on." They ran through the castle until they came to the tapestry.

Moving quickly, they slid behind the tapestry and opened the door. Once again, they groped their way down the pitch-black tunnel to the end and pounded on all the stones around the door until it opened. Together, they burst into the hidden room and ran to the ornately carved wardrobe, pulling on the handles.

"Shakespeare must have locked it!" Diana cried. "Then he disappeared with the key."

"Wait, I have a tool." Matt dug his hands in his pockets and pulled out a small screwdriver. "I was using it this morning to finish the decorations. I'll just slide this into the lock and . . ." He jiggled the tool in the lock. Nothing happened.

"What's wrong?" Diana asked.

"I don't know. I thought I could pop a spring in the lock," Matt replied.

"Do locks this old have springs?" Diana asked.

Matt sat back on his heels and sighed. "I'm not sure. Now what do we do?"

"There's only one thing we *can* do," Diana said. "We've got to go find Shakespeare."

Chapter 3
A Midnight Swim

*M*att peeked out from behind the tapestry and saw no one in the hall. "Come on," he said to Diana. "We'll sneak out of the castle and head toward London. Then we'll find Shakespeare, get the key, and go home." They walked carefully down the hall.

"Oh, there you are, Lady Diana!" Diana cringed. Lady Overdone charged down the hall toward them. "This hair simply is not done up properly," she fretted. "Attempt it another time. I must look perfect when I greet the queen."

Diana whispered fiercely in Matt's ear, "Get that key *soon*!" She forced a fake smile on her face and turned to Lady Overdone. "Certainly, Lady Overdone," she said.

Matt kept going quickly down the hall and located the front door. He ran through the busy courtyard and out the wide, iron front gate.

For now, he knew exactly where to go. His choice was simple, since there was only one dirt road leading away from the castle. The sun shone brightly, but he was still cold. He wondered where he would sleep tonight. Lord Overdone had sent him out with no thought to his safety or comfort. *Servants weren't very well treated in these times,* he thought.

After several miles, he saw a boy pulling a cart. "How do I get to London?" Matt asked him.

"At yon fork in the road, turn to the left," the boy replied. He turned and pulled a heavily woven cloak from a pile of them in the cart. He offered it to Matt. "You are in need of a covering, are you not? My mother weaves these herself."

"I have one farthing, but I need to buy food," Matt told him. "What's a farthing worth, anyway?"

"There are four farthings to a penny, of course," the boy said. Matt put his head in his hands.

"What have you to trade? Those boots, perhaps?" the boy went on.

Matt looked at his feet. He'd never be able to walk for two days without his boots. He dug in his pockets and pulled out his screwdriver and his student photo I.D. card. He really hated to part with the screwdriver. He might need it again on this trip. But he also needed to stay warm. He held out the I.D.

The boy snapped up the photo I.D. "This is a most amazing painting that you carry. What great artist could render such detail in so small a space? I must have it!"

The boy had obviously never seen a photo before. No one had, Matt realized, since the camera hadn't been invented yet.

21

"Sure!" Matt said, quickly returning the screwdriver to his pocket. "Go for it!"

"How strangely you speak," the boy commented as he tossed the woolen cloak to Matt. Matt smiled, realizing that he sounded as strange to people of this time as they sounded to him.

He pulled on the cloak and let its warmth surround him. "Thanks a lot," he told the boy. "Enjoy the, uh, tiny painting."

"Farewell," the boy called as Matt walked on ahead of him. The first golden rays of sunset were tinting the sky when Matt felt his stomach rumble. He also shivered and knew he had to find a place to spend the night or he would freeze.

A mile more down the road, he met a young girl. Matt told her he was traveling on business for Lord Overdone. "Could I sleep in your barn tonight?"

"My mother will shelter you for the night," the girl said. Her mother turned out to be a widow with six children.

"Oh, you are all on your own," the woman said. "Come in and share our meal." She refused to take Matt's farthing, so he repaid her hospitality by using his screwdriver to pry open a stuck cabinet. She let him sleep on the floor.

In the morning, Matt ate a little gruel with the family, then thanked the woman and continued on his journey. She insisted on pressing a thick piece of bread into his hands as he left.

This day was even colder than the one before. After hours of walking, Matt was hungry and his feet ached. He watched a farmer go into his house for his noontime meal, and then he sneaked into the man's barn. Cows mooed at him as he ate his bread and helped himself to some water from a bucket.

Feeling much better, Matt forced himself to return to the road. By late afternoon, he came to a fair set up in a field. His stomach roared at the wonderful smells of food.

Matt wandered through the fairgrounds, looking for someone who was selling bread.

"Win a tasty leg o' mutton," a man shouted. "Knock over the pins and win some mutton!"

What was mutton, anyway? It didn't matter. The mutton meat was roasting over an open flame, and it smelled great. Not far from the flame, eight small pins, like bowling pins, were set up. At home Matt played baseball, and everyone said he had a good throwing arm.

"I'll try," he said to the man.

"That will be a ha'penny," the man told him.

"I will pay one farthing to play this game," Matt said. He attempted to sound confident and bold.

"Be gone, beggar!" the game man shouted.

"I am no beggar. I have *plenty* of money," Matt bluffed. "But I will pay only one farthing to win a mere leg of mutton."

From the corner of his eye, Matt noticed three ragged men listening to him. Their narrowed eyes and low whispers made him nervous.

"Be off with you!" the man running the game said. "Show me a ha'penny or go!" With a sigh, Matt inhaled the succulent smell of roasting meat and walked away.

It was growing dark, and the fair's vendors were packing up their wares. Matt walked on down the road. The moon rose, and he began to think he should find somewhere to spend the night, no matter how hungry he was. Then he heard footsteps crunching behind him, and he whirled around.

Three figures were standing in the moonlight—the three men who had been watching him at the fair. "Give us your fortune," one of them demanded.

Matt struggled to keep his voice from quavering as he dug out his farthing and addressed the robber. "This is all I have, and you are welcome to it." He stepped forward to give the thief the money, but the man slapped it from his hand onto the ground.

"I want the entire fortune. The one you boasted of!" The other two men stepped forward and sneered.

"Really, I don't have a fortune," Matt said.

"Get him!" one of the men shouted.

Matt raced away with the three men chasing him. He wished he had his sneakers on instead of heavy boots as he ran down a sloping hill and into a forest. Zigzagging among the trees, he tried to lose them in the darkness, but they stayed doggedly on his trail.

Matt emerged from the woods and saw a wide, moonlit river. One of the men burst from the woods. "Got him now!" he called to the others as he blocked Matt's way along the river's embankment. A second man blocked his way in the other direction, and the third man prevented him from running back into the woods.

Matt looked desperately around. There was only one way to escape. He plunged into the icy river.

Chapter 4
Swept Away

Matt gasped for breath as the icy current dragged him along. Normally, he was a good swimmer, but he couldn't raise his arms because the heavy, wet cloak pinned them down. The sodden wool was growing heavier by the moment, pulling him under the water. Struggling, he untied the cloak and shrugged it from his shoulders.

Instantly it became easier to move, but the water felt even colder. As enormous chunks of ice floated alongside him, he grabbed hold of one solid slab and boosted himself up on it. It buoyed him above the turbulent river for nearly a mile.

Up ahead, on the river, Matt saw flickering lights. Dark silhouettes moved across the river, as though the people were walking on the water.

I'm in shock, he reasoned. *This freezing water has affected my brain, and I'm imagining things. Stay alert,* he encouraged himself. *Don't lose your mind. It's all you've got right now.*

He shook his head to clear it, but when he looked again, the lights and men were still there. The closer he got, the more distinctly he could see them. They were carrying long planks of wood, and they *were* walking on top of the water. "Help!" he shouted, just in case this wasn't some kind of hallucination. "Help me! I'm here, in the water!"

One of the men pointed at him. A few minutes later, a low rowboat appeared at his side and two men dragged him up and into the boat.

"Forsooth, this lad is nearly drowned," one said to the other. He tossed a heavy blanket over Matt. "Let's get him in front of the fire with all good speed."

The boat carried them to a part of the river that had completely frozen over. The men hadn't been walking on water. They'd been walking on ice! They were carrying heavy timbers on their shoulders.

As the men helped him from the boat, Matt wanted to thank them. His teeth chattered so badly, he couldn't form words. On shore, they wrapped him in another blanket, gave him some stew, and told him to rest by a roaring blaze.

The fire had been built beside a large, round building. Matt watched as the men moved about him, throwing tall shadows in the firelight. The ripping sounds of wood being torn from the building filled the air. "Excuse me!" he called to a man passing by. "What are you doing?"

The man crouched beside Matt. His face glowed in the firelight as he grinned. "We're tearing down this place. It's called the Theatre. It's stood here for more than 20 years, but now it's coming down."

"Why?" Matt asked. "For that matter, why are you doing it in the middle of the night?"

"Here is the tale," the man said. "The landlord owns this land, but not this building. He will no longer lease the land to the Theatre's owner. So the owner hired a carpenter to loosen the boards. Now we actors and our friends are here to carry the timbers across the Thames River, where we will use them to build a brand-new theater." He broke into loud, uproarious laughter. "Imagine the landlord's face when he returns to his land in spring and finds the Theatre gone!"

"What will happen then?" Matt asked.

The man stood. "I don't know what will happen to him. He'll probably collapse in a state of shock and rage. But we will be building the greatest theater the world has ever seen." He pointed across the half-frozen Thames River. "It will be right across there in Southwark, outside of London."

The mention of London reminded Matt of his mission. "Do you know where I could find William Shakespeare?" he asked.

"I certainly do," the man replied, standing. "He's out there on the river. Even the great playwright himself is carrying timbers across the river. Good news, he's coming right toward us."

Matt climbed up to his knees and saw Shakespeare on the river. So this was the urgent business he had to rush off to! Matt waved and Shakespeare waved back.

Then he was gone! Once again, he had completely vanished!

"Zounds!" the man beside Matt shouted. "The ice has broken! He's fallen in!" He raced toward the river, shouting, "Broken ice! Man below!"

Matt arose, too, and hurried toward the ice. He got out onto the river in time to see Shakespeare's friends hauling him up out of the water. Matt pulled off one of his blankets. "Here," he offered.

In minutes, Matt was once again in front of the fire, sitting beside a shivering Shakespeare. "So, m-my friend, what b-brings you here in the d-dead of night?" Shakespeare asked through chattering teeth.

"A couple of things," Matt said. "I'm Matt, by the

way. Okay, first: Lord Overdone needs you back at the castle, because the queen is coming. He wants you and your actors to put on a play for her. But what's really important—at least to Diana and me— is that I need the key to the time portal. We want to go home."

"Oh, forgive me, my dear friend," Shakespeare said. "I didn't consider that when I locked the portal—I simply locked it from habit. Of course you may have the key." He patted his waist. Slowly an anxious expression overtook his face. He stood, searching the ground. "My pouch! The key was in the pouch that I keep around my waist. But it is not here!"

He picked up a stick of thin timber and lit it in the fire. Using it as a torch, he traced his way back to the river, searching the ground as he went. Matt followed by his side, also looking for the pouch.

"It must have come loose when I fell into the Thames," Shakespeare decided. "Oh, this is a tragedy. Some of my greatest plays have been inspired by my travels through time. I traveled back and met many of England's greatest rulers. I have returned in time to ancient Rome and to Verona and Venice in their glorious pasts. I had hoped to meet Cleopatra and Mark Antony, but now all that is lost. Oh, woe is me."

"Excuse me," Matt said. "But woe is *we*. Diana and I can't get home now. What will we do?"

"Learn to love this time," Shakespeare suggested. "It is a most fascinating time to be alive."

"I suppose," Matt said. "But my time is fascinating, too, and I want to get back there—not be a Renaissance kid. My family and Diana's will go wild looking for us. Besides, poor Diana is stuck there with that horrible Lady Overdone."

Shakespeare sighed deeply. "Yes, Lady Overdone is a bit much." He stood. "Help us to pull down this theater, and tomorrow my acting company and I will return with you to the castle and see what can be done to diminish the suffering of poor Diana."

Matt wasn't looking forward to this. How could he tell Diana they were trapped in the Renaissance for the rest of their lives?

Chapter 5
Queen Elizabeth

Oh, Matt, please get back here with that key soon, Diana thought. She looked down at her hands. They were red from all the pins and barrettes and creams she'd been putting in Lady Overdone's hair for two straight days. The woman had changed hairdos at least ten times! Even though Diana was supposed to be a royal lady-in-waiting, she was little more than a servant.

Today, she'd awakened in her cold bedchamber, under her skimpy blanket, to the sound of Lady Overdone screaming. The woman had burst into the room and shouted that she'd had a dream that told her that her hairdo wasn't flattering. Diana couldn't believe how cold the castle was—and she *really* couldn't believe how obnoxious Lady Overdone was.

"Perhaps another of your ladies might do a better job," Diana suggested.

Lady Overdone scowled at her. "I *have* no other ladies at the moment. They *all* leave me, though I know not why. I treat my ladies so well, yet they are never grateful. One even sneaked away in the middle of the night dressed as a washerwoman."

I know why that lady snuck away, Diana thought as

she quickly dressed in her Juliet costume. *It's because you were the most annoying person she ever met!*

Diana decided to try a hairdo she'd done for her older sister's prom. She heated tongs in the fire, used them to curl Lady Overdone's hair, then piled ringlets high on her head. She used fistfuls of some bad-smelling grease that Lady Overdone used as styling gel to smooth the hair in front.

"It's the latest look," she explained. "This hairdo is very in style this year, you know, because of the Latin invasion."

"Latin invasion?" Lady Overdone cried, alarmed.

"It's an invasion of music," Diana explained.

"Oh, yes. The explorers have been importing so many things. For the last hundred years there's been no stopping them—and now music. It was bound to happen," Lady Overdone said. "So you're saying this is a Latin hairdo?"

"Uh, that's right," Diana replied, and Lady Overdone smiled, obviously thrilled. She left seeming very pleased, and Diana crossed her fingers, hoping that this was the last hairdo she'd have to create.

Diana shook out her stiff, weary hands and walked to the window. She set her elbows onto the windowsill and laid her head in her hands, gazing out into the courtyard. No one had arrived yet at the castle—not Matt or Shakespeare or the queen. She saw no one moving through the courtyard other than the servants who worked at the castle.

The door creaked, and she whirled around toward the sound. Matt stood in the doorway. "You're back!" she cried happily. "I didn't expect to see you so soon. The queen hasn't even come yet!"

Matt entered the room and Shakespeare followed him in. "I wouldn't have been back until tomorrow except Shakespeare and his actors got a lift with some fishermen who were bringing their catch down the Thames. They brought me along with them."

"I know a back entrance into this castle, and we used it to come in," Shakespeare added. "We do not wish for the Overdones to know of our presence just yet. Sometimes I think they should have been named Lord and Lady Overbearing."

"That's for sure," Diana agreed. "Did you bring back the key to the portal?"

Neither of them answered, and the unhappy expressions on their faces made Diana anxious. "You have it, right?" she said. "I mean, Mr. Shakespeare, you had it, and now you're here. So it's here, right?"

Matt and Shakespeare shook their heads. "Sadly, it fell into the Thames when I had an unfortunate tumble into the river," Shakespeare explained. "'Twas the only one of its kind, too. Another clever device of Leonardo's."

"No!" Diana cried. "This isn't happening!"

"Lady Diana!" an all-too-familiar voice bellowed from down the hallway. Diana rolled her eyes and sighed miserably.

"Quickly, let us away to see what we can do about the time portal," Shakespeare said to Matt.

"Just deal with her for now," Matt said to Diana. "We'll be back as soon as we can. Maybe we can open the wardrobe somehow." He held up his screwdriver and grinned. "I still have this, after all." He waved as he and Shakespeare disappeared out the door.

In an instant, Lady Overdone came in, obviously quite excited. "Her Royal Majesty, Queen Elizabeth, has just entered the courtyard with her entourage of royalty and servants. This is too thrilling! Forsooth, I shall faint!"

Please don't faint! Diana thought, panicked.

Instead of fainting, Lady Overdone sat down at a table with a mirror. "I'll need you to help me powder my face. I hear the queen powders her face to hide her terrible skin. Of course, it's just a rumor. Powdering has become all the rage in London. Everyone always wants to look like the queen. I wonder if she wears a wig. If she does, I shall have to get one."

"Good idea!" Diana said. "I think you should just shave your head and get a wig. You could get a thousand wigs, all in different styles. You'd look even better than the queen."

"No! No!" Lady Overdone said. "One cannot look better than the queen. One must only seem to be in the style of the queen."

"Whatever you say," Diana said. "But think about getting those wigs!"

"Now you must help me cover my face with white powder," Lady Overdone insisted.

"Do you have powder?" Diana asked.

"Oh, heavens, no. I know, Cook has flour. That will do." She took a good look at Diana. "First, put on that new dress I gave you. We can't have you disgracing the household. Then, get some flour from Cook, and hurry. I must be ready to greet the queen looking my finest."

Diana went back to her chamber to change, then hurried toward the kitchen. She entered the busy room that was full of chatting servants and good smells. Meat turned on spits over fires in huge stone ovens. A large pile of fresh fish flipped and flopped. Some women sang a song as they rolled out huge slabs of dough. It seemed to Diana it would have been better to have been mistaken for a kitchen maid than an attendant to a vain, demanding woman.

A middle-aged woman approached and curtsied. She was wearing a long dress, apron, and cap. "What can I do for you, lady?"

"I need some flour for Lady Overdone."

The servant hurried to a cabinet and took out a large burlap bag. "Here you go, m'lady," she said. She handed Diana the bag, and then curtsied again.

Diana smiled at her. "Thanks a lot." She hurried back down the hall, holding the heavy bag of flour. If she didn't get this to Lady Overdone quickly, the woman would probably be in a state of frenzy. Diana picked up speed, dashing rapidly around a corner.

Suddenly—*slam*! She bumped into someone. The impact caused her bag of flour to fly up into the air. It opened, spraying flour everywhere . . . then landed on none other than Queen Elizabeth herself!

Chapter 6
A Desperate Move

"Oh, wow!" Diana cried. "I am so sorry!" Then she took a closer look and realized whom she had hit with a bag of flour.

"Oh, no," she muttered. She'd seen the queen's picture often enough in her textbooks to recognize her. Queen Elizabeth was very distinctive.

Not too many other women had that same high forehead and bright orange, curly hair. Lady Overdone had been right about the powder, too. Even though the queen was covered with flour, Diana could still tell that she had a ton of powder on. There wasn't a chance Diana could have overlooked the sparkling, diamond-and ruby-encrusted crown. It now sat at a decided tilt on the queen's flour-covered head.

The queen's attendants surrounded her and glowered at Diana. She wondered what it would be like to have her head chopped off. But the queen smiled and straightened her crown. "You have lost your bag of flour, young lady."

Queen Elizabeth's attendants hurried to brush flour off her elaborate pleated and beaded dress. Flour drifted from the huge, round collar.

"I am so sorry, Your Majesty," Diana repeated, curtsying. She reached over to help dust off the queen's dress. "Really, I didn't mean to . . ."

A man pulled her away harshly. "How dare you touch Her Royal Majesty! Guards, seize her!"

"There is no harm done," Queen Elizabeth interrupted. "I'm sure the flour attack was wholly unintended."

"Oh, it was completely accidental, Your Majesty," Diana gushed. "I'd never dump flour on you on purpose. It's an honor to meet you."

"Just so," the queen said.

Shakespeare came up to the queen. "Your Majesty," he said, greeting her with a sweeping bow.

"Oh, good playwright, how fare thee?" the queen replied, smiling fondly at Shakespeare.

"I fare well," Shakespeare said. "I see you have . . . uh . . . met Lady Diana." He glanced at the flour-filled scene and shot Diana a questioning look.

"Can I be of help with this mishap?" he asked.

Queen Elizabeth smiled. "No, it is a mere trifle. What play will you perform for me tonight?"

"It will be a play I wrote some years ago. It is one Your Majesty has not yet seen, and one that has proven to be most popular with audiences. It is called *Romeo and Juliet*."

"Oh, that's a good one!" Diana said.

Shakespeare grinned. "I am so glad you find it to your liking, Lady Diana."

Lord and Lady Overdone appeared and took in the scene. "What has happened here?" Lady Overdone shrieked. "*What* has—"

The queen stopped her by raising her hand. "Let us not make much ado about nothing. No harm has been done."

Lady Overdone looked at Diana angrily, but Lord Overdone smiled at the queen. "As you say, Your Grace. Now let me escort Your Grace and your entourage to the finest wing of our humble castle so that you may refresh yourselves. Tonight we will feast. The cook has prepared fine fish just caught in the Thames for dinner."

He strolled down the hall with Queen Elizabeth and her attendants. Lady Overdone scowled at Diana and then hurried to join her husband. "Did you get the wardrobe opened?" Diana asked Shakespeare.

"Alas, no," he replied. "Matt is still there working on it. You may be destined to spend the rest of your days in England, but perhaps we can arrange for you a better fate than serving Lady Overdone."

"I hope so," Diana said. "But what I really want is to go home. I mean, no offense, but I don't want to live in the Renaissance for the rest of my life. I was hoping to be an actress, but you don't have movies. I suppose I could act on the stage in one of your plays."

Shakespeare shook his head.

"Why not?" Diana cried. "I'm pretty good."

"It is no matter how good you may be. Women are not allowed to appear on stage."

"What!" Diana cried. "Who plays Juliet?"

"Boys play the part of women," he informed her.

"That's terrible!" Diana said.

"We have actors who are very skilled at playing women's parts," Shakespeare told her. "Come and watch us rehearse. The lord and lady will be busy with the queen all day, and 'twill take your mind off your troubles."

For the rest of the day, Shakespeare worked with his actors to prepare their production of *Romeo and Juliet*. Diana and Matt watched, fascinated.

"Remember," Shakespeare told his actors. "This *appears* to be a story about young love. It *appears* to be a tale of two young people who are mad with love, who cannot be together because of their opposing families. But this is not what the play is about!"

"It's not?" Diana asked. It was what *she* thought the play was about.

"No, it is about fate—about two star-crossed lovers who are fated not to be together. They are doomed by destiny."

"Sounds familiar," Matt commented. "Would being doomed by destiny be something like if you were minding your own business when some guy from the past got you sucked into a locker and then trapped in another time, far away from your home, family, and friends?"

Shakespeare turned red with embarrassment. "Yes, that sounds much like a person who has been doomed by destiny."

"I thought so," Matt said.

Shakespeare sighed, then went back to his play. Matt and Diana left the rehearsal and walked through the halls.

"I guess we're really stuck," Diana said.

"I guess so," Matt said unhappily. "At least we have each other. If I were here at the Overdone's castle by myself, it would be a lot worse."

"It *would* be worse," Diana said. "But being here at all is pretty bad. Maybe we could leave with Shakespeare or with the queen when she goes.

Anything would be better than staying here."

That evening Diana entered the large banquet hall along with Lord and Lady Overdone. Three tables had been set up in a U-shape.

The Overdones walked in with Diana and took seats at the middle table. Diana had to admit that everyone looked very nice in their fancy clothes. Two other higher-ranking members of the Overdone household also joined them.

Soon members of the queen's party were sitting at the middle table, too. One seat in the middle was left empty. Diana realized she would be sitting near Queen Elizabeth herself.

Many men and women of noble blood from nearby

estates had been invited to this feast in the queen's honor. They walked in and sat at the other two tables. A platform had been set up in the middle of the tables, where Shakespeare and his company of actors would perform the play.

Soon everyone was seated except the queen. When she walked in, everyone stood. Diana was pleased to see that she'd gotten all the flour out of her hair.

Queen Elizabeth wore a gown even grander than the one she'd worn that afternoon. She nodded graciously at Diana as she passed her. The mark of recognition made Diana feel proud, and she lifted her chin a little higher.

When the queen sat down, she waved her hand, indicating that it was all right for everyone else to sit. Then a line of servants filed in, each holding some part of the dinner. One servant carried a big platter of fish. Matt held a large plate piled high with baked potatoes. Diana smiled and dared a small wave to him as he passed.

The queen was served first, and all the servants stood in line waiting to fill her plate. A huge fish, complete with its head, was deposited on her plate. One of her servants approached with a large knife, and with it, he split the fish down the middle.

Along with everyone else in the room, Diana watched the servant cut the fish. But not everyone noticed what she had seen. Something gleamed golden inside the fish.

Could it be? Diana thought. *Probably not; it might just be a fishhook. What are the chances, really? Still . . .*

Curious, Diana leaned forward so she could see past Lord and Lady Overdone.

The servant removed the fish's backbone. That seemed to be when the queen also noticed the shining object. She plucked it from inside the fish and turned it in her heavily-ringed hand, inspecting it.

There was no doubt about it. After all, it was the work of Leonardo. There was no other like it. It had to be the key to the wardrobe.

In a second, Diana was up from her seat. Climbing over Lord and Lady Overdone, she knocked them backward. The servant tried to block her path, but she pushed him out of her way. That key was her only way home. She had to get it, no matter what it took!

Two more servants tried to grab her, and she jumped up onto the table to get away. "Matt!" she shouted. "It's the key! It's here!"

The queen stood and stumbled back as Diana grabbed the key from her hand. "Sorry, Your Majesty, but I really need this," Diana apologized.

"Guards!" Lady Overdone screamed at top volume. "Seize Lady Diana! Get her!"

Chapter 7
The Last Chance

*D*iana struggled with two guards as they attempted to grab her. One of the guards pulled at her arm, and the key flew from her hand. Matt threw himself at it with his best slide-into-home-base lunge. "Noooo!" he shouted as the key slid past his outstretched hand and disappeared beneath the table.

He looked for the key, but all he could see below the table was feet. It had to have fallen into a floorboard, he decided. He stuck his fingers into the gap separating one plank from the next. There was no sign of the key, though.

Diana wrenched away from the guards and jumped down to the floor next to Matt. "It's down there somewhere," he told her. She knelt with her eye to the crack in the floor, but all she could see was darkness.

A guard pulled her up abruptly. "What would you have us do with this troublemaker?" he asked Lord Overdone.

"Take her to the dungeon!" Lady Overdone boomed before her husband had the chance to answer. "First she attacked the queen with flour, and now she has yet again made an attack on the queen. Take her friend, too. He plays a part in this plot against Her Majesty. Both of them will rot there for their insults to Her Royal Highness!"

"As you wish, my lady," the guard said. With his other hand, he grabbed Matt. Matt struggled to get away, but it was no use.

Queen Elizabeth stood. "Halt and desist!" she shouted in a voice so commanding that everyone in the room froze. "Guard, unhand these young persons." The guard loosened his grip on Diana and Matt. "Lady Diana, I demand that you explain your actions."

Diana breathed deeply, trying to collect her thoughts. What she said now could make the difference between being free—or spending the rest of her days in some moldy, old dungeon. Her words not only affected her future, but Matt's, as well.

Did she dare to tell the truth? Would the queen believe it? Diana decided to find out.

"Your Majesty," she began, trying to keep her

voice from trembling. "My friend and I have been brought here from the future by William Shakespeare. He used a time travel machine that was most probably invented by the great artist and inventor Leonardo da Vinci. We need that key to get into the machine and return home."

She stopped to take another deep breath. "It seems Mr. Shakespeare dropped it in the Thames, and your fish, your dinner, must have gobbled it up. I was astonished to see it on your plate! I was trying to retrieve the key just now so Matt and I could journey forward in time, and get back home."

The queen stared at Diana, who smiled anxiously at her. She could see that the queen couldn't quite believe what she had just heard. It *was* a pretty unbelievable story, even though it was all true.

To Diana's astonishment, the queen returned her smile. Diana glanced at Matt. What if she *did* believe them? What if she commanded the Overdones to rip up their floorboards and find the key?

Before the queen could speak, Shakespeare rushed into the banquet room. "Pray tell, what is the problem here? Allow me to intercede on behalf of my two young friends. They mean no harm to anyone!"

"Sir!" the queen said. "This young woman has just told me a most preposterous story of time travel and a missing key. Is there any truth to this?"

"By all means, yes. Forsooth, it is all true," Shakespeare confirmed. "I merely wanted to show them our glorious time—a time in which art, literature, and science have been reborn. A time that will someday call Queen Elizabeth the greatest monarch ever to rule England."

The queen's eyebrows rose in surprised delight. "Will history truly record me as such?"

"It will," Shakespeare replied confidently.

"I suppose you know this because you, too, have been traveling through time?"

"Exactly, Your Highness."

Matt and Diana watched her closely. What would the queen do next?

"The greatest monarch ever to rule England," she repeated. "I like it."

Matt and Diana turned to each other hopefully. "She likes it," they said at the same time.

The queen clapped her hands in delight. "Allow me to congratulate you, Master Shakespeare. You have staged this entire event in an attempt to interest me in your next play; one that I presume is about the notion of time travel. A play about traveling through time is indeed an ingenious concept."

Matt stepped forward. "The key is still under the floorboards," he said, afraid they were forgetting his only way home.

"The key, yes!" the queen said. "You inserted a key in my fish to keep the drama going, and then made sure Diana and Matt grabbed it lest I choke. Brilliant!"

"No, no, the key's for real, Your Majesty," Matt insisted. "It's not just a prop. We need it."

"There is no need to keep up this charade any further," the queen assured him. "I have thoroughly enjoyed it. Now let us continue dining, and we will see this *Romeo and Juliet*."

Matt returned to Diana. "Well, the good news is we're not spending the rest of our lives in the dungeon."

"The bad news is that we're never going home," Diana said. "Not unless we find that key."

As she spoke, Shakespeare's fellow actors came out onto the stage. "We will now present the tale of two star-crossed lovers, *Romeo and Juliet*," Shakespeare told the audience. "In this production I, the play's author, will play the part of Capulet, Juliet's father."

"Well, at least I'm going to see Shakespeare in a play!" Diana said. "The next thing we have to figure out is how to find that key. I don't think things are going to be too great for us here once Shakespeare and the queen leave."

"Good point," Matt agreed.

The play began, and all the lords and ladies grew silent. Diana and Matt had seen the high school production of the play last year, but it had been nothing like this play.

These actors spoke the words naturally, and their actions were easy to understand. Matt and Diana soon forgot that Juliet was being played by a boy and became completely involved in the story. When Juliet awoke and found that Romeo was dead, everyone in the banquet room was crying, even Lady Overdone.

As the play ended and the company took their bows, Queen Elizabeth stood and applauded. Lord and Lady Overdone and all their guests did the same.

"I commend you, Master Shakespeare, on a most marvelous play," Queen Elizabeth said.

"Many thanks, Your Majesty. I hope Your Majesty will come see us in the new theater we will soon be building. It will be called The Globe Theater because, after all, all the world's a stage."

"That it is," the queen murmured. "That it is."

Diana joined Matt in a corner. "I have an idea," he told her. "I heard the queen's people saying they're leaving first thing in the morning. If we don't find the key, why don't we sneak out of here with them?"

"Good idea," Diana agreed.

Everyone in the banquet room rose as the queen stood to walk out. Matt and Diana squeezed against the wall as she passed.

The queen was nearly out the door when Diana noticed the ruffled hem of her elaborate gown. She jabbed Matt hard in the side. "Look!"

The key hadn't fallen into a crack in the floorboards at all! It had slid all the way under the table to where Queen Elizabeth had been sitting. Now it was being dragged out the door, caught in the hem of the queen's gown.

Without speaking another word, Matt and Diana dove for the key. The queen felt a tug on her dress and stopped short.

"They are at it again!" Lady Overdone shrieked. "'Tis a plot against Her Highness! Guards! Don't let them get away!"

Diana and Matt scrambled to their feet. "Run!" Matt shouted.

Diana bolted away. She and Matt raced down the long hallway. They both knew where they were heading: to the tapestry that hid the entry to the wardrobe.

"Halt, varlets!" shouted one of the guards. Five of them chased after Diana and Matt.

The friends raced through the halls, sliding around corners. "Down there! There!" Diana said, clutching at Matt's shirt to stop him. She'd spied the tapestry at the end of a long hall.

Matt glanced back and saw the guards charging toward them. He pulled Diana behind an empty suit of armor that stood in the hall. They barely dared to breathe as the guards thundered past them.

They ran down the hall, ducked behind the tapestry, and pulled open the door behind it. Moving hand over hand, they went down the dark hall as fast as they could manage. *Bang!* Matt hit the right stone to open the door on his first attempt.

The wardrobe opened easily when they inserted the key. They stepped inside.

"Okay! Let's get out of here," Matt said. "What do we push to get back to our time?"

"Wait!" someone shouted. Shakespeare stood in front of the open door. "You cannot depart yet!"

Chapter 8
All's Well That Ends Well

"I always lock the door from the inside when I travel," Shakespeare told them. "If the door opened mid-trip, heaven knows where it might dump you out. Imagine spinning through time and space for all eternity."

"Okay, we'll lock the door," Matt said.

"But then you'll have my key, and I'll be able to travel no longer. I have the solution. I will travel forward in time along with you, deposit you safely home, and then return with the key."

"Fine," Diana said. "Hop in."

Shakespeare jumped into the wardrobe and locked it. Then he pushed down a small brown lever nearly hidden in the upper corner.

All at once, the air inside the wardrobe began to glow with swirling colors. Matt and Diana once again had the strange sensation of tumbling through space with their molecules not quite all in one place.

Finally, with a thud, they crashed into the narrow locker. "Ow!" Diana yelled. Matt's elbow was pressing painfully into her ribs.

"Grant me one favor," Shakespeare requested as

they stepped out of the locker. "Don't tell anyone of this. I wish to make future journeys into your world."

"We won't tell. Who would believe it?" Matt said.

Down the hall, Mrs. Hill came around the corner and walked toward them. Diana and Matt saw that she was still in her costume. They heard noise from the cafeteria. "The fair's still going on!" Diana said. "I wonder how long we've been gone. Just a few minutes, I bet."

"Great costume," Mrs. Hill told Shakespeare. "Matt, is this your father? I've never met him."

"Indeed, dear lady," Shakespeare said. "This boy is as a son to me. Now that I've seen your delightful fair, I must depart. I have work to do here in your lovely town. Parting is such sweet sorrow."

"But *Father*, I thought you were going directly *home*," Matt reminded him.

"I have changed my mind," Shakespeare said. "Do not worry, I have my key firmly in hand." Shakespeare waved and walked jauntily down the hall. The kids waved back as they watched him go.

"What a charming man," Mrs. Hill said. "Now, why don't you two come back inside."

"We'll be right there," Matt told Mrs. Hill. "I have to get something from my locker." Mrs. Hill nodded and went on her way.

"I want to get something to put in this locker for Shakespeare to find when he comes back," Matt explained to Diana.

"What is it?" Diana asked as they neared Matt's locker. "All you have in there are books."

Matt opened the locker and pulled out a thick atlas. "This has maps of the whole world," he said. "With this, Shakespeare will always know exactly where he's going when he time-travels."

They placed the book in Shakespeare's time portal locker. Then they went inside to the fair. Mrs. Hill was standing by the replica of the Globe Theatre.

"Shakespeare was such a genius," Mrs. Hill said. "It's amazing how much he knew. It's almost as if he had some mysterious way to travel through time and space."

Matt and Diana just looked at each other and grinned.